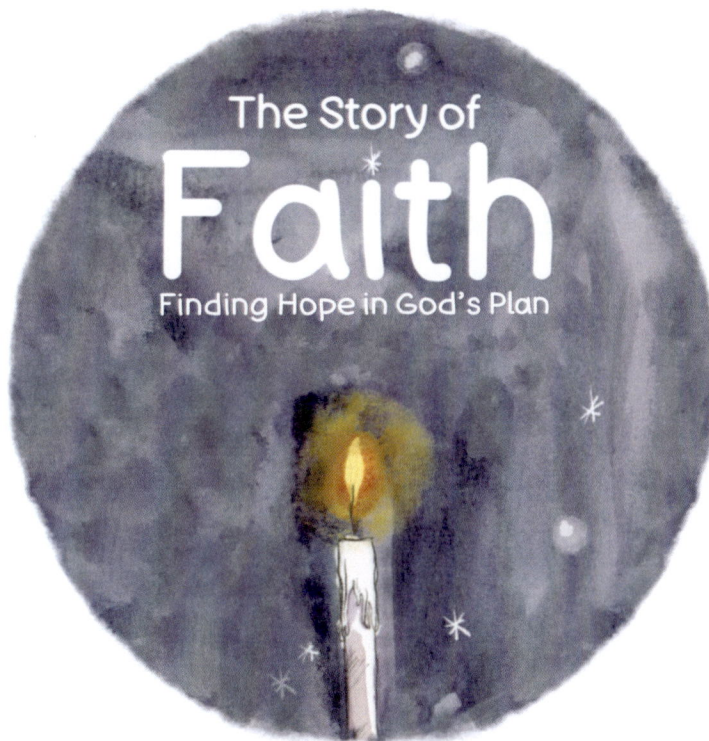

The Story of
Faith
Finding Hope in God's Plan

Story By Jannine Koert
Illustrations By Krystal Kramer

STORIES AGAINST STIGMA

Story Copyright © 2024 by Jannine Koert
Illustration Copyright © 2024 by Krystal Kramer

www.storiesagainststigma.ca.

ISBN Paperback 9798325103056

Book Dedication

Faith wishes to dedicate this book to her Almighty King for restoring her from darkness to light, at a time she was ready to give up - Jeremiah 29:11.

While Faith's story is grounded in the context of her religious experiences in rural Nigeria, Stories Against Stigma recognizes that survivors of pervasive social stigma are incredibly resourceful. Faith's resilience is largely informed by the religious and spiritual influences that have supported her throughout her life.

Therefore, Stories Against Stigma also dedicates this book to Faith, and the millions of other survivors who are still searching for a hope-lit path.

—

By purchasing this book and sharing it with friends, you are helping to financially empower Faith, so that she can reach her dream of becoming a journalist. Faith has no limits on the future she envisions for herself.

Faith was a bright little girl growing up in the dense jungles of Nigeria.

Faith loved to do many things. She loved running across the one logged bridge to meet her friends in the village.

She loved helping her mum with carrying vegetables back from the garden.

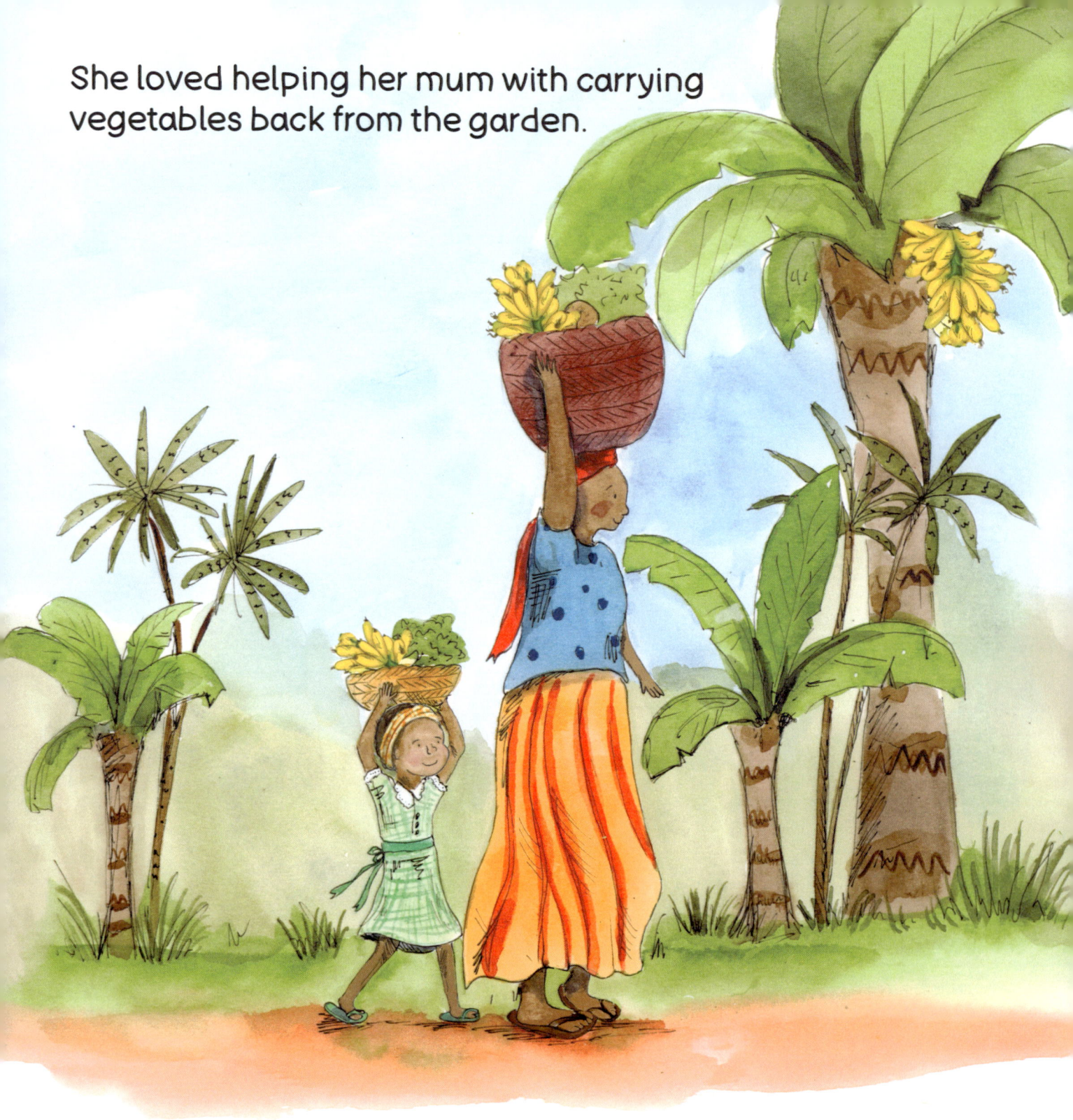

She loved to sit down after a long day and read her Bible with her mum at her side.

Most of all, she loved going to school. She loved walking over the bridge, across the village, and up the steep hill to school with her friends.

But one day, Faith got really sick and was never able to walk again.

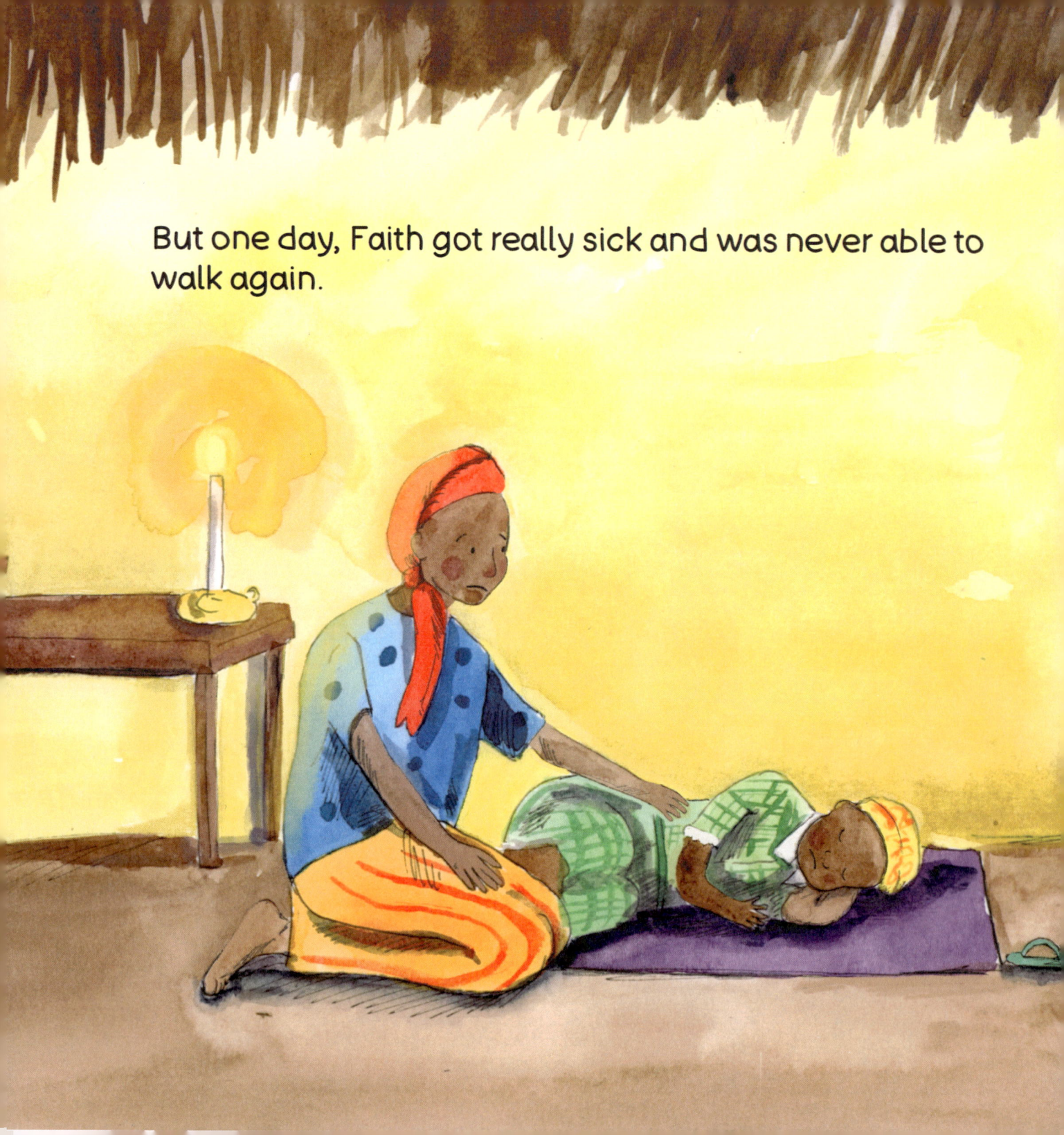

She could no longer cross the one logged bridge on her own because she was too unsteady. Her friends would run ahead of her to school because she was too slow.

Her mum started to carry her on her back, over the bridge, across the village, and up the steep hill to school.

At school, no one would talk to her. As the months passed by, Faith grew lonely and sad.

$2 + 2 = 4$

$10 + 10$

$4 + 3$

But then, something even worse happened. Faith's mum got really sick, and passed away. Faith was all alone.

Faith was sent to live with her aunt, but no one loved her like her mum did. People looked at her like she was cursed and sent her away.

One night, she asked God, "Why are all these bad things happening to me?"

She heard God whisper back and say, "I know the plans I have for you", just like her mum used to read to her from the Bible.

I know The plans I have for you

One day, a strange woman came to her village. She spoke to Faith about a special school, where children like her would be loved for who they were.

Some kids could walk, some couldn't. Some kids could talk, some couldn't. Some kids could see, some couldn't.

Faith was brought to the new school where she was given a wheelchair. She was quick to make new friends, all of whom were excited to bring her along on their adventures.

Faith also learned to draw. She spent all of her free time drawing pictures of her new life at school.

One day, a girl named Jannine came over from a faraway country called "Canada". After Faith shared her story, the girl asked, "Faith, what has made you so strong?"

Faith gave a big smile and said, "I give God the praise. He knew the plans He had for me. He is the one who has helped me."

A Personal Note from Faith*

My name is Ejeh Nkemjika Faith. I am from Ebonyi State in Nigeria. Life has been good to me. I was not born a cripple. It was the work of the devil that I suddenly stopped walking in 2006. My mother supported me, but fell sick in 2011 and passed away in 2018.

I remember a time when I was sick with typhoid fever, after I was already unable to walk. No one thought I would recover again due to how sick I was. At the time, my mom or myself did not have money. Nothing. This is when my mom got sick. My sister was asked to give money to help me, but she refused saying, "what if she dies after spending money on her?" My pastor kept praying, assuring everyone that I was not going to die. Everyone found it difficult to believe I would survive.

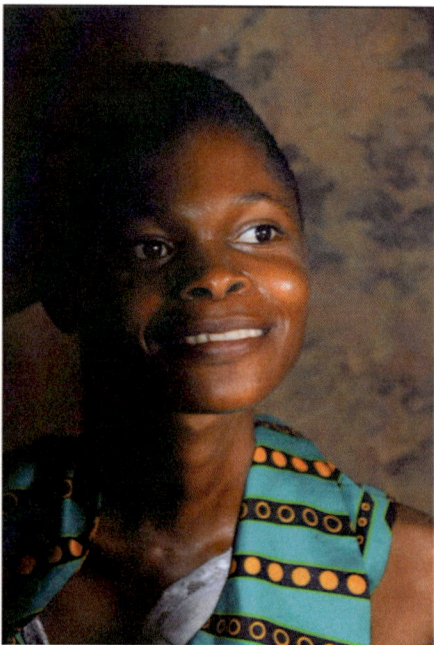

Today, I still tell the story. It is not by my own power but by the grace of God that I live today. A man of tomorrow will never die today. The work God assigned to me is not done.

A year after that, I had a dream where white people were walking around me with light, both male and female. Other white people were cooking rice, serving people free of charge, and houses were being built with a different style. When I woke up, I prayed over it, and kept it to myself, because I had never been near white people, let alone had them in my midst.

At that time, I would often dream about furthering my education. I had already graduated from primary school, but my family was unable to afford secondary school.

A month later, a lady I didn't know came to my house. I was helping a neighbour with their homework assignment. She saw me and asked if I would like to further my education. I said yes, but that I didn't have a sponsor. The lady said okay, and then related the issue to the founder of a disability-inclusive school. The founder accepted me, free of charge, and I soon became one of those studying in secondary school in 2016.** I was afraid that the devil would one day hurt me, ignore me, and drive me away.

One day, God sent me an unforgettable daughter by the name of Jannine to Nigeria. All of my burdens were carried away automatically. For example, my favourite food is rice, and I have not lacked it since.

This reminds me that when God says yes in your life, nobody will say no since God is speaking. I had a dream again where I was putting on a [post-secondary] uniform. I prayed about it, and kept it to myself as usual. In February of 2023, after seeing my [graduating] grades, my pastor congratulated me and said he will register me for the JAMB exams.*** To the glory of God, I passed the test! Please pray for me, I would like to further my education. I have a dream of becoming a journalist.

I thank each and everyone of you who show support and are concerned about my situation. I pray that God will see each of you. I never thought an orphan like me would find favour amidst people who are supporting me now. I say, may the Lord who did it for me, remain exalted through you both now and forever! Amen! ***

Footnotes:
* These are Faith's words, as an allied organisation is it one of our core values that they are shared with you in their entirety
** More than 50% of Nigerian girls are not attending primary level education, and even less make it to secondary school. On top of that, 95% of children with a disability in Nigeria have no access to education.
*** The JAMB is a Nigerian entrance examination board for post-secondary institutions.

www.ingramcontent.com/pod-product-compliance
Lightning Source LLC
Chambersburg PA
CBRC100736150426
42811CB00070B/1907